The Seven Year Promise

Pressed, Processed, & Polished for the Promise

LaTasha Houston

All rights reserved. No portion of this book may be reproduced in any form without permission from the author or publisher, except as permitted by U.S. Copyright law. The use of short quotations or occasional page copying for personal or group study is permitted and encouraged.

Scripture quotations are taken from the Holy Bible, New Living Translation, copyright ©1996, 2004, 2015 by Tyndale House Foundation. Used by permission of Tyndale House Publishers, a Division of Tyndale House Ministries, Carol Stream, Illinois 60188. All rights reserved.

Printed in the United States of America
ISBN: 9781733759717
Published by: Awaken U Publishing

Table of Contents

Prologue v

The Prayer Room...vii

Introduction xi

The Waiting Room...xiii

Chapter 1: The Plan 1

The Locker Room... 8

Chapter 2: The Pain 11

The Patient Room.. 21

Chapter 3: The Promise.................................. 25

The Study Room 36

Chapter 4: The Perspective 39

The Conference Room.................................... 49

Chapter 5: The Purpose.................................. 53

The Meeting Room... 72

Chapter 6: The Preparation............................ 75

The Training Room 90

Chapter 7: The Perfection 93

The Operating Room 109

Chapter 8: The Promotion 113

The Board Room 133

LaTasha's Room 136

About the Author 143

Stay Connected 145

To my mom,

Thanks for always being my constant supporter and my example!

Prologue

I will like to point out that God wrote this book. When I say He wrote it I'm not talking about the cliché and extra Holy response of me "being so full of faith and obedience that I let Him lead me in everything in life and I didn't disobey or waver." No! I literally mean that one day in my quiet time with God He revealed to me that I am supposed to write a book. I was like oh ok. A book was not in the plans but it was not far-fetched considering the fact that, that's what I do in my blogs— writing. However, I just didn't understand what I would write about. I figured that later I would think of something to write about, just like I did with all my blogs.

However, God threw a boomerang when He revealed the title. He told me to title the book "The Seven Year Promise" and He told me to start it now! I was truly stuck when He said this because I didn't know what I could possibly write about with this topic. So, I ignored Him. The problem was the idea was keeping me up at night and I was getting excited to write the book although I didn't know what to write about. It was a battle between my flesh and my spirit. My flesh was saying "Girl you know what you were promised 7 years ago through prophecy; however, it looks nothing like it now so don't you start that book and disappoint yourself!" My spirit, on the other hand, was saying "You know what He promised you 7 years ago so just start writing the book in obedience and FAITH. He has to be working something out in the background if He dropped this book in your spirit."

As you can see, my spirit won! I just started putting an outline on paper. The idea was to start slow and subtle so if disappointment started to creep in it wouldn't be hard to quit. I had a name for each chapter (with no content) in just 30 minutes. It came to me like osmosis. It was as if God was just waiting for me to pick up the pen. After the chapter titles were solidified, I started writing "The Plan" chapter because I knew I could go on and on about my plan. On the contrary, the one chapter I knew I could not touch at all was "The Promotion." I had no idea what it was, what it entailed, or how it was going to happen. Now, here we are with an entire book less than a year later.

The Prayer Room

Before starting this book, let us pray for your heart and your spirit to be in the right place sis. Let us pray for you to be open to receive whatever God speaks to you through this book. I touch and agree with you that you are going to get all that God has for you.

Sis get to writing...

What made you pick up this book?

What were you hoping to get out of this book?

What are you praying for right now in your life?

x

Introduction

Sis,

Before you start reading, go get the prettiest, thickest journal you can find. I say this because I am adamant about writing out my feelings, emotions, thoughts, and whatever speaks to my spirit at certain times and in certain moments. I journaled my way through this entire process that you are about to read about in this book. Writing through it allowed me to process it all and be honest with myself about how I felt. It is my journal so I didn't have to worry about writing in such a way that I could not be honest with myself. I wrote out the good, bad, and ugly. I was REAL with myself.

Also, a journal allowed me to go back and read over old passages to see how far I had come. In these times, I was able to reflect on my growth and recognize why it was so important not to repeat certain behaviors. Reading and reflecting allowed me to see how much the first mistake either robbed me of my peace, caused turmoil, or added confusion. These past entries were reminders to myself to not be the one to take my own growth away from me.

So, I invite you to do the same. WRITE IT OUT! As you go through this story of a piece of my life, take notes of what speaks to you and why. Write out what the Holy Spirit says to you. As you read through my mistakes, if something is relatable, sort through your emotions on paper by writing it all out in your journal. Sis, you are going to be so surprised at your growth when you go back and read through these entries.

Lastly sis, this is me sharing what God put on my heart to disclose about my journey. However, I could not neglect to add the Word of God to this book. I made sure to add instances from the Bible that relate to whatever story I am telling from my own journey. There may be some moments you may have to pull out your Bible to read the full story, as I did when I was writing this book. So, be sure to keep your Bible handy too.

Happy reading sis!

The Waiting Room

Sis, have you ever been in a position where you were waiting on God? If no one else understands you, it is me! You will see when you go through and read this book. I put all my thoughts on paper, raw and unedited.

Sis, get to writing...

What are you waiting on God to do?

Why are you waiting?

How are you waiting?

When you honestly sit and think about it, are you waiting on God or is God waiting on you? Is there something He told you to do but you have not moved on it yet?

Chapter 1: The Plan

> *Proverbs 16:9*
> *A man's heart plans his way, But the LORD directs his steps*

plan
/plan/

noun
1. a detailed proposal for doing or achieving something.
2. written account of intended future course of action aimed at achieving specific goal(s) or objective(s) within a specific timeframe.

verb
decide on and arrange in advance.

The most important things to remember in this definition are:
   1. Intended.
   2. Specific goal or objective.

3. ***Specific timeframe.***
4. ***In advance.***

The Plan

Since a little girl, I always intended to have my dream life. It was decided in advance that I would get married then have children. Part of that could be centered on natural instincts as a girl and the other part solely because I am southern and that's what southern women do—become someone's wife. The goal was to live in a nice house, have an awesome career, with a loving husband, and live like the Joneses (whoever they are). Later the objective would be to add children to the equation. I pictured myself having the house, career, and husband by the timeframe of 25-28 and adding children to the equation by 30-33, after my husband and I had thoroughly enjoyed our time to ourselves. That was the plan—the intended, the goal and objective, and the specific timeframe—that was decided in advance, by me.

If you have not noticed by the way I just laid out my plan, I am a planner. I try to plan most of everything—down to my days, my activities, etc. So, it would be no different when it came to my life. Based on this, it should come as no surprise that I like it when things go according to (my) plan. A plan makes events and happenings dependable, consistent, and somewhat predictable (for me). When I have an idea of what's going to happen, it gives me a sense of security. In other words, I like to feel in control of my life. When things happen how they are supposed to happen—supposed to means the way I planned it—I feel more secure and confident. I then feel like I can tackle life head on. For that reason, when it came to my life, my plan was to carry out the plan—which was my plan.

As life continued to unravel, I started to notice the biggest problem with my plan was that I can't control everything. The other problem I noticed is that most of the time, when we make plans, we aren't really the ones who control their outcomes. Sure, we can do our best to try and make them happen but so much of our world—and our lives—are dictated by things outside of our control. No matter how hard you try, how good you are, or what you do, there are simply some things that you just can't control. On top of that, not every change is a result of

YOUR (things YOU can control) actions. Some things just catch you off guard and send you into a tail spin because they aren't what you expected or wanted and you can't control it.

Although the Bible is full of stories of people who encountered change of plans, I never considered the chance of my plans being changed. I know that after the glorious exodus from Egypt, the Israelites were "supposed" to walk into the Promise Land. However, after 39 years of wandering in the wilderness, it was clear, things were not going as they had planned. I know that Mary and Joseph were "supposed" to get married, start a family, and live "normal" lives but, after an angel showed up with a mission from above, plans changed. I know that Lazarus was "supposed" to be healed; after all, he was a close personal friend with Jesus Himself. However, after his sickness took a turn for the worse, suddenly his family realized, plans had changed. Nonetheless, none of this forewarned me or prepared me for the possibility of my changed plans. Of the plenty moments from the Bible of where one thing was "supposed" to happen but it didn't, I still thought I had everything under control. Even in reading and knowing the Word, I never imagined that it would happen to me. I got hit and didn't see it coming. Even worse, I wasn't prepared to fight this spiritual warfare.

Like the many infamous stories in the Bible, I encountered things in life (to some degree) that weren't "supposed" to happen. Like many of the characters in the Bible, I didn't understand why God had so drastically changed the plans. In my plan, I was supposed to be married by now. I was supposed to be promoted by now. I was supposed to have achieved years of marriage with my husband by now. In my plan, there was no back up plan in case things didn't go as planned. So, when the plan didn't go as planned, I had an unplanned breakdown.

Plans can be good but, when our focus is so intent on making them happen, it can be crushing when things just don't work out the way we wanted them to. Too often, our lives are dedicated to serving our own plans. As Christians, we are called to serve only one

Master and, if we are not too careful, our plans can become idols. The plan taught me that life is unpredictable and some things are just beyond my control. At moments I had to learn to not hold tighter to what I wanted. I had to learn how to let go of my grasp of control on my life and let God in. Until my plan failed, I had never been at a point where I was not truly able to control a situation or at least play a major part in the outcome. That's when it hit me that God is more concerned with the outcome than the scenario. After all, the scenario is only temporary but outcomes are eternal. The Israelites did find the Promise Land after 40 years. Mary and Joseph raised Jesus Christ Himself. Lazarus was brought back from the dead after the illness took his life. The moral of the story is, life happens! Plans change. God is still there. Since God is still there, even out of such a difficult circumstance, a change in plans can still be used for good.

The Locker Room

You have made the team and you are now in the locker room. It is halftime and your team is down by a few points. The coach looks at you since you are a starting player and wants to know why you are not following his lead. He called a couple of plays and, instead of you going along, you ran your own play. He wants to know what your initial plans for this game were and why you felt you couldn't trust him, as the coach, to follow his lead.

Sis, get to writing...

The Plan

What are some plans you initially had for your life that didn't go the way you planned?

Are there some plays that you know God called but you chose not to go through with? If so, why?

What generational curses are you trying to break, if any?

Chapter 2: The Pain

> *Job 6:1-3*
> *Then Job spoke again: "If my misery (pain) could be weighed and my troubles be put on the scales, they would outweigh all the sands of the sea. That is why I spoke impulsively."*

pain
/pān/

noun
mental suffering or distress.

verb
cause mental or physical pain to.

The most important thing to remember in this definition is:
1. *Mental.*

By the age of 27, I had all of these minus one. The one thing I was missing was ironically the one thing I thought was the most important ingredient to the recipe... piece to the puzzle... key to the lock. This missing piece made me a statistic. This missing piece changed the dynamic of my life. This missing piece interrupted my entire plan, causing me indescribable pain. This had me asking the question, "How did I go from planning for a family to being a single mom?"

By the age of 27, I had two of four things in my plan. I was living in Washington, DC. I had been in my career with the Federal Government for five years. Oh, and now I also had a child. Too far from my plan and so close to the pain, I couldn't seem to find a middle ground. I was in a relationship that didn't feel like love at all. I was confused and not sure how to get things back to a good place. I knew I was nowhere near where I wanted to be but I couldn't figure out exactly how to get to there. I was in such an unknown season. It was a season where God seemed silent and my plan for the future seemed lifeless. I didn't plan this – the life I had. It was supposed to be different. I was left confused and disappointed. I suddenly realized that the love I wanted and the love I had just wasn't the same. This type of love was not a part of my plan.

I remember one day—before I birthed my child but while in this relationship—being so drained that I just dropped to my knees and started crying and praying. When I say crying, I am not talking about the silent tears that roll down your face. I am talking about the type of cry that is loud and deep. It was as if my soul was weeping for all that I had allowed myself to go through within the last year or so. It was bottled up and I finally let it all out. I cried out to God literally for this first time in my life, while literally saying the words aloud "God help me." I cried out to God asking for guidance and expressing every piece of pain I felt. I remember saying the words "if you tell me he is not the one for me I will walk away today." For the first time, I had truly invited God into my relationships, into my life, into my plan, and, most importantly, into my pain. I cried myself to sleep and it was a peaceful sleep. It was peaceful because I let it all out and I knew God heard me. For the next few days the only thing I could think to do was to seek God more. There was no more I could do for the relationship and, quite frankly, I didn't even know how to help myself. I surrendered. It was a natural surrender because I was tired. I was tired of trying to figure it out.

When our whole lives are shaped around our plans, suddenly we can become so concentrated on accomplishing them that we lose sight of God. I sacrificed so much to get to my plan, to include sacrificing my relationship with God. This cost me. It cost me my identity, my worth, and my peace. I spent years feeling like the Israelites—trying to get to what was promised to me. I was going around the same (relationship) mountain and never made it to the Promise Land. I was living my life trying to achieve the plan that I determined was right for my life. I was continuously putting my plan over God's plan.

Instead of acknowledging God is in control and

seeking Him, I eventually tried to manufacture my own peace. Again, I was attempting to maintain control instead of turning to the one who was in control. I was coping daily instead of using my one-time escape, **God**. I was spiritually numb... wondering where I was in life, how did I get here, and where was God!!! Above all, I was stuck and didn't know what to do next. I had no idea what His will was at this point – at the most vulnerable point in my life!! Day after day, sermon after sermon, prayer after prayer, I was discouraged and frightened by a widening gap between my desired/planned life and my real life.

I felt the devil knew just what to test me with based on what I prayed about the most. Take Job in the Bible for instance. The devil knew where to test Job because he prayed about what he feared the most daily—his children falling short. ***Job 1:4-5 Job's sons would take turns preparing feasts in their homes, and they would also invite their three sisters to celebrate with them. When these celebrations ended—sometimes after several days—Job would*** *purify his children. He would get up early in the morning and offer a burnt offering for each of them. For Job said to himself, "Perhaps my children have sinned and have cursed God in their hearts." This was Job's regular practice.* He prayed about his children's possibly sin against God daily and, just the same, I prayed daily for my husband. My fear was always never to be a single mom or a woman who didn't marry, due to my family being full of unmarried women. I wanted to break the generational curse. I wanted it to end with me. In Job 1:7 the devil admits to watching everything: *"Where have you come from?" the LORD asked Satan. Satan answered the LORD, "I have been patrolling the earth, watching everything that's going on."* I felt like the enemy was patrolling, listening, and watching to know what area to test in my life. It was definitely an easy one like Job because it was the area I prayed about the most—MARRIAGE! Subsequently when the test came, my pain and frustration came from trying to do something about a situation I couldn't do anything about. If you would have asked me then the cause of my pain and frustration, I would've told you that it was because things were taking too long to manifest. Now, I recognize that the pain and frustration was caused by me trying to make something happen instead of waiting on the Lord to bring it to pass. My pain and frustration were signs of me acting independently and it broke me down.

It was in this brokenness, when I had nothing else to cling to, that I realized that I did not have many answers. The one answer I knew with certainty was that I needed to go back to what I did know...God! I knew His Word was full of promises and that His word would never return void. Therefore, it wasn't that I was seeking the (abundant) life that was not due to me. It was that the more I tried to do it my way the more the promises became unclear. At this point, I needed to reassess where I was in the process to get to the promise. In order to pass the frustration test, I needed to let go and trust God to do what only He could do. I had to let God be God. At my breaking point, I took a deep breath and exhaustedly handed Him my clean slate.

The pain taught me that when things started to get "out of control", I had to make a deliberate choice to no longer hold tighter to what I wanted and what I expected. I had to make a deliberate choice to release my expectations and embrace what is. For me, it is—I have amazing children with full operation of their limbs who are very healthy. We didn't want for anything or stand in need of anything. Most importantly, I had to change my perception of my now life as a single mom. My current status did not mean I was stuck or that my children were doomed to misery.

The pain also taught me to rid myself of self-righteousness. In some instances, I felt like I was suffering just as much as Job. Granted, I didn't completely lose everything but I surely felt like I did. My life felt shattered and in shambles. The sentiment I shared along with Job was suffering and not understanding why. In my opinion, I was a good person. I intentionally did good. I never mistreated people. I went to church. I paid my tithes. My intentions were good. My question now was, "Why me?" just like Job. Obviously,

Job was a good servant. He wasn't tested because of how "bad" he was. Job 1:8 says ***"Then the Lord asked Satan, "Have you noticed my servant Job? He is the finest man in all the earth. He is blameless—a man of complete integrity. He fears God and stays away from evil."*** Therefore, God basically offered Job for testing because He knew Job would pass. Although both Job and I passed, we both questioned God's actions through the majority of the process.

During the process, my faith was based on my feelings in that moment. I was allowing my emotions to determine my beliefs. God ultimately wanted me to trust that He knows what He is doing in me. In the midst of the testing, Job was still sustained. Although things were taken from him, he was sustained. The same was true for me. I am now cognizant when moments like this come and I can acknowledge it is a trust test. The test is learning to trust God when we do not understand what is going on. Many will take the easy route at times like this by going back to what they were used to, something that is easier and quicker. At times I did and ended up back in the same emotional/broken cycle. So, the key is to keep walking with God and don't turn around. I learned that even through the pain, no matter what I am going through, God still had the same plan for me then that He had for me when I was born. He never changed His mind. From the instant the enemy attacked me, God had my restoration in mind. Now I look back at those moments and I say the same thing that Job said in Job 42:5-6, *"I had only heard about you before, but now I have seen you with my own eyes. I take back everything I said, and I sit in dust and ashes to show my repentance."* The pain was a required experience so I could truly appreciate what it means to be kept and fully rely on God.

The Pain

The Patient Room

You have been having extreme pain. You have tried everything you can to alleviate the pain but it is not working. You decided to make a doctor's appointment to get the pain checked out. You walk into the doctor's office and the doctor asks you a few questions.

Sis, get to writing...

How long have you been in pain?

What caused your pain?

The Pain

What are your symptoms?

How have you been treating and addressing your pain up to this point?

The Seven Year Promise

Chapter 3: The Promise

> *Habakkuk 2:3*
> *… This vision (promise) is for a future time. It describes the end, and it will be fulfilled…*

prom·ise
/ˈpräməs/

noun
1. a declaration or assurance that one will do a particular thing or that a particular thing will happen.

2. an indication that something specified is expected or likely to occur.

verb
assure someone that one will definitely do, give, or arrange something; undertake or declare that something will happen.

The most important things to remember in this definition are:

1. *Declaration.*
2. *Expected.*
3. *One will definitely do, give, or arrange.*

Here are a few truths: we are all human; we all make mistakes; and we all do things we regret. Another truth is, although God loves us and doesn't hold them against us, we are still faced with consequences. The good thing is if we rely on God, not our own ability to make our plans, things that weren't supposed to happen actually turn out all right. God allows second chances if we allow Him to take us through a process to restore and heal us from encounters that we were never meant to have.

It became easier to stand on the hope of things being restored when God gave me a promise. In the previous chapter, I told you about me crying and praying, which ended in a natural surrender. Well, the next week I received a call from a mutual friend telling me she had a dream. She first explained to me that she has visions through dreams often and she was finally getting to a point where she was accepting her spiritual gift. She told me that she spent days trying to suppress the dream she had about me but God gave her no peace. So, the only thing left for her to do was to be obedient and tell me her dream. She stated that in the dream I was crying and praying at the altar, similar to what I was actually doing that night in my room. She recanted every ounce of my prayer. It was my first encounter with someone having a vision and "prophecy." I was scared and relieved at the same time. I was scared because I had never witnessed such a godly encounter and relieved to know that God not only heard me but answered.

She and I kept in touch and she later invited me to a revival at church. It was at this church that I had my second godly encounter… the Pastor was a prophet. When the prophet called me to the altar to give me the prophecy assuring me of marriage, he also told me God was about to bless me with a gift. At the time of my visit what I did not know was, I was pregnant. I am not talking about spiritually pregnant with a dream or vision but literally and physically pregnant. A baby was in my belly!

I was finally able to witness first hand receiving a "word from God" the way I had always heard people talk about. The problem was that no one ever told me how the promises of God worked. No one ever told me that if He speaks something, although it is guaranteed to happen, it is not guaranteed to happen immediately. When God revealed the promise, I became excited and hopeful for my future. The promise made a situation that looked unsalvageable now look like what the Bible describes as "*what was meant for evil being used for my good.*" This refreshed my faith. To me, the promise was a sign of a turning point and that I was headed towards victory. However, I had no idea I still had to wait.

The thing is I never expected the promise to come immediately. However, "so close" to me meant at least within a year or so. More than anything, it meant that I would at least start to SEE something that mirrors the promise soon. Needless to say, that was not the case. The wait started to trigger memories from my failed relationships. Since in previous relationships, men had broken promises, to me this promise was no different. It wasn't that I doubted the Prophet but that the last man who promised me something broke that promise. Those broken promises left me with trust issues, which heightened my control issues even more. I started feeling this need to jump into action and help myself. When I let my guards down and tried to let a man be a man, in the relationship, I was left feeling empty. Therefore, I was back to protecting myself again because I felt I could do it better than anyone—to include God.

Although my prior control issues were not due to being hurt, the pain heightened my need to control situations. I felt had I continued to exercise control I would've also been able to control my feelings, control the situation, and, most importantly, I could've controlled the outcome to a certain extent. Consequently, I started to blame myself for being foolish enough to let go of the control in the first place. Then the pain started creeping back in. The pain had me not believing in the promise because my trust issues, at this point, were so bad that I didn't even feel I could trust God. I was so focused on my current problems that I forgot there was a promise attached to it.

The planner in me jumped into action. I received His promise but it was taking too long to manifest. Naturally, I started developing my plan to make it happen. When things got wacky, I never did a true pulse check to get instructions or to see if I was on the right track to get to the promise. Just like other things in my life, I jumped into it thinking I knew how to make the pieces fit. Moreover, I thought I knew how to get the last piece of the puzzle. I was doing everything within MY control—doing HIS will MY way. For once I understood Sarah, Abraham's wife.

God gave me a promise like He did Sarah. He told Abraham that they, in their old age, would bear a child (Genesis 17). Sarah got tired of waiting for God's promise to come to manifest. Sarah decided to see if her handmaid, Hagar, would conceive a child by Abram (Genesis 16:2). She came up with a plan for God's promise. Although God had promised Abram a son by Sarah (Genesis 17:16), Sarah convinced herself that Abraham having a son with Hagar could be God's way of giving her the child she was promised. Sarah doubted the promise God had given her, the same way I started to doubt after a while. She couldn't see it in the natural realm so it took over her ability to see it in the spiritual realm. It took over her faith to believe that God was able because of her current circumstances. Hence, came Ishmael—Abraham and Hagar's son. Slowly, this became LaTasha's story. It seemed that after I received the promise, my situation had gotten worse instead of better.

Although Hagar and Abraham conceived Ishmael, it was not the child promised to Sarah and Abraham. Isaac was their promised child. Sarah and Abraham waited another fourteen years before Isaac was conceived. I often wonder if it takes us so long to receive promises because once we give birth to the "Ishamels" in our lives we must deal with the consequences. We want to carry out our own plans and then we want God to bless them. We often settle for the "Ishamels" of life when God had an "Issac" planned for us. I wondered if that was my story of why what was once a "so close" turned into a "is it still going to happen" moment for me!

The current year reminded me so much of prior years of my life when I was in this same cycle. Suddenly, it hit me that I was back in the same place I was before He gave me the promise. I felt like I was getting the firsthand experience of "if you didn't get the lesson the first time, He will take you through it again and again until you get it!" Welp, here I was again... *sigh*! This made me ponder how many YEARS had I wasted trying to get to the promise. How many YEARs did I do my own thing, which probably kept me from the prophecy? The initial pain that I described in the last chapter was a result of me not receiving God's promise according to my plan/vision. The pain that was creeping in now, however, was the regret when I pondered the opportunities and doors that had been opened but I bypassed them for what I perceived as "better". The "better" stemming from the belief that I could do it all or create it all for myself.

Regardless of what I thought it was going to be or what I thought it should have been, God is a God of making things what they are supposed to be. However, He could only do that if I invited

Him in instead of still trying to stick to my own plan. God was basically asking me, "Do you want my promise or your plan?" It hit me so hard because I thought my plan was His promise and this is mainly because I blinded myself to His will. In opening my eyes, I realized that if my plan was His plan, I would be God. He says plainly in scripture, "Your thoughts are not my thoughts and your ways are not my ways." However, I came to term with the fact that, although it was not His plan, I am still qualified to receive His promise. Now, I had to allow God to get me back on track to His promise. In order to do so, the first step was to surrender and stop fighting for my plan.

The promise taught me the true meaning of Habakkuk 2:3... ***This vision is for a future time. It describes the end, and it will be fulfilled. If it seems slow in coming, wait patiently, for it will surely take place. It will not be delayed***... in my seven-year process. The prophecy was God's way of having me to look at life and see it with new eyes. It was to show me the mountain top to remember while I was going through the valley. It was to give me hope for the future. It was to remind me that the process had a purpose, which was to ultimately get me to the promise. Although, there was not a body or a face in that "husband spot," there still sat the existence of what God promised. This is what He wanted me to use as hope during the times when I was the only parent showing up for my kids' functions, patience during those lonely nights, strength for those tiring days when I was having to get off work and immediately chauffeur children to different activities, and, most importantly, as fuel to fight the enemy when he came for my thoughts trying to convince me that my life would always be this way.

The Study Room

Sometimes we have to put everything to the side and just go back to what God said. The way we know what God said is by reading His Word. Today I encourage you to find a bible verse that speaks to you and/or your situation and write out what the verse(s) means to you. Do not be vague with phrases like "oh God wants me to have faith"! NO! Truly write out what it means for you just as I just did for Habakkuk 2:3.

Sis, get to writing...

The Promise

If you need help finding a verse or topic, maybe go to my blog, pick one to read, and write on it. I always include scripture throughout my blogs.

The Seven Year Promise

Chapter 4: The Perspective

> *Isaiah 55:8-9*
> *"My thoughts are nothing like your thoughts," says the LORD. "And my ways are far beyond anything you could imagine. For just as the heavens are higher than the earth, so my ways are higher than your ways and my thoughts higher than your thoughts.*

per·spec·tive
/pərˈspektiv/

noun

a particular attitude toward or way of regarding something; a point of view.

The most important things to remember in this definition are:
    1. Attitude.
    2. View.

I felt like Mary, mother of Jesus, pregnant with a promise but no idea if it would happen. Pregnant, no husband, single mom, how could this be God's plan for me? Was I still the one He gave the promise to? It didn't look like a favor at all. I really questioned if there was any purpose in this journey, any purpose towards the daily trudge to a promise I could not see and didn't understand. I am sure Mary wanted to stop a million times but she went. She walked, she rode, she traveled on this path to the place God wanted her to be. She did it and so did I, even though on some days I wanted to stop.

Sometimes the journey doesn't make any sense. Sometimes the journey hurts. Sometimes it seems to come at the worst possible moment. I know because I have been on that road—the road to "Bethlehem," following God's will! I know what the life of submitting to Him but life still being hard is like. It can be confusing and painful. Furthermore, sometimes, in these moments, God doesn't intervene. He doesn't always step in to make it easy. However, in these moments, He calls us to keep walking. He also calls us to start trusting.

I felt I had done so much to try to make the prophecy come true that I was so far out of the will of God and I felt there was nothing He could do with me. Although I was continuing on with the routine of life, work, taking care of children, going to church, etc., I felt there was no way he could truly get me back on track. I was convinced I had missed the opportunity to be a wife. I was lost and felt so far away from my plan and His promise. Now what do you do when you always felt that at the very least you could fall back on either your plan or God's but now both felt unreachable?

I was waiting, planning, and hoping. Of all of these, I was planning more than anything and really only had a little ounce of hope left. Not to mention, I wasn't waiting properly. I was merely waiting while waiting—waiting for God to move, waiting for God to act, and waiting for God to change my circumstance. All I truly wanted was for God to change everything to get me back to my plan and every day that passed with no sign of that I became even more frustrated. Have you ever experienced "buyer's remorse" after choosing to trust God when you're too far to turn back, but too close to give up? This was me!

Frustration usually does one of two things. Frustration either drains you completely to the point where you get defeated or frustration births the desire for something different. I chose the latter. It was not like before when it was just me depending on me but I had children at this point. I had little eyes looking at me for an example. I can't really remember how it happened. I just know that at some point, during the wait, my perspective shifted. It was at this moment that the promise was no longer torture to me but reassurance.

A light bulb turned on one day and I realized that God gave me the vision before He gave me the struggle because the vision was to be my weapon during the struggle. When you remember what God had in mind you can fight the struggle. This helped me to understand that the fight with the enemy was over my vision not the marriage. The enemy wanted me to become blind to what God spoke and operate in the flesh. I said to myself, "The vision is tarrying but I am going to wait for it." I had to remember that God loves me, so He didn't give me the vision to torment me while I wait or to one day revoke His promise. When it felt like torment I had to keep in mind that the vision is ultimately stronger than the struggle because the vision had God's power, favor, provision, and endorsement on it. Therefore, though I felt struggle in this season, I had the promise that it was going to bring my victory in another. God is not a man that He shall lie.

Once I shifted to a victory mindset, I had to become intentional about no longer focusing so much on the future and stay in touch with myself—in the present. I had to let go of the picture of what I thought life would be. This included accepting my life where it was today and stop wishing for tomorrow. Most importantly, I had to exercise control by not jumping into planning mode. I allowed myself to grieve the old picture that I had in my head. This allowed me to acknowledge it in a healthy way and not just bury it. After I acknowledged and grieved it, I decided to stop being stuck in the past and gauging my future against it. I told myself that from that day forward I would stop repeating, rehashing, and reliving moments in the past.

The changed perspective taught me to not let my expectations of how life "should be" blind me to the beauty of the life I was living. I stopped wishing away time waiting for "better times" ahead but instead started appreciating where I was now. I had come a long way and I was still learning and growing. My past taught me many lessons that I am thankful for. I took those lessons and started making the best of things in the present. The best philosophy to be coupled with that is accepting what you can't change. Accepting that life is unpredictable and at times, out of control, allows you to move forward. If you don't accept this truth, you keep fighting hopelessly against reality. You remain caught up in the suffering and struggle of trying to control, fix, and change what you can't control, fix, or change. More effort, more perseverance, or more attempt to control won't always create the outcome you seek. The best perspective to commit to memory is that you may not be able to change the situation or other people, but you can change how you react and think. The second part of that is also committing to memory that no longer striving to fix the situation is not giving up or giving in. In the past, this would make me feel weak and like I was passively accepting what the other person gave me. Essentially, I thought it was their win and, ultimately, my loss. The perspective shift helped me to realize that I had more control when I allowed myself to only put my effort into what I could actually control. This perspective also made me change my definition of a win.

Before the perspective shift, I had stopped serving, giving, and praying the way I needed to during that time. My relationship with God was stagnant and not growing so technically I wasn't growing. My growth was stunted because I was mad about my plan not working out. I was mad that I was in this situation that was never a part of my plan. Even worst, I was mad because it seemed He gave me a promise to dangle in my face for torture. As my perspective continued to change, the more my desire to get closer to God grew.

Since I couldn't control or change my situation, I threw myself into the person that could—God. I signed myself up for an 18-month long commitment. I joined a ministry that helped me to study the women in the Bible. I felt like a student going back to school to learn. I was on a journey to learn more about God and, in the process, I learned more about myself. Suddenly, I started going to church more often, reading my word other than on Sundays, and being intentional about having a true relationship with God. I no longer wanted to worship, read, and obey just out of obligation of what I was "supposed to do" but because I truly had a relationship with God. I now had the desire to do what made Him happy. It is no different than you honoring a friendship with one of your good friends. If you know something hurts her feelings, makes her sad, or she doesn't like it, you would try your best to honor that. I wanted to do that for the "friend" who knew everything about me and had my best interest at heart. The other part of that was I also wanted my behaviors, thoughts, and patterns to become like His without much thought or hesitation. I wanted to know His ways and have them become my ways, naturally.

By the end, like Saul, I was pleading for forgiveness. 1 Samuel 15:24 says, ***"Then Saul admitted to Samuel, "Yes, I have sinned. I have disobeyed your instructions and the LORD's command, for I was afraid of the people and did what they demanded. But now, please forgive my sin and come back with me so that I may worship the LORD."*** My perspective changed and I regained my identity as God's daughter. Sometimes as parents, we parent our children in a way that transforms their hearts right after severe hurt has befallen them. With the same thing in mind, God wasn't out to hurt me or punish me. He was attempting to use this situation for my good. First, however, I had to go through the process of rebuilding me because I had no idea who I was anymore. It was a process of re-knowing God and gaining a deep foundation for our relationship rather than it being built off scripture alone or what other people had told me about Him. In this process I found someone that I never want to lose again... ME!

The Perspective

The Conference Room

Sis, I called you in for a conference because I want to talk to you about where you are currently. As a woman who was honest with herself about where she was and now has a changed perspective, I want to help you elevate your perspective. It is time for you to start looking at things from the perspective that God sees.

Sis, get to writing...

What are the pieces of you that you've tucked away? What are you not saying? If Jesus was sitting in the room, since He is all knowing, what would he say?

What are you currently upset with God about?

The Perspective

Write out some things that you are grateful for right now!

What distractions do you need to eliminate to have a mindset shift?

Chapter 5: The Purpose

> *Romans 8:28*
> *And we know that God causes everything to work together for the good of those who love God and are called according to his purpose for them.*

pur·pose
/ˈpərpəs/

noun
1. the reason for which something is done or created or for which something exists.

verb
1. have as one's intention or objective.

The most important things to remember in this definition are:
1. ***Reason.***
2. ***Objective.***

I compared myself to Saul because at one time I disqualified myself from purpose.

1 Samuel 9:21 Saul replied, "But I'm only from the tribe of Benjamin, the smallest tribe in Israel, and my family is the least important of all the families of that tribe! Why are you talking like this to me?"

After exiting toxic relationships and getting to a point where I was just mentally drained, surprisingly, the last thing on my mind was a relationship. Although I wasn't healed from it, the pain was starting to ease. Christians are always proclaiming there being "purpose in the pain" right? While I was ready for the pain to end, I am not so sure I was ready for the "purpose." I wasn't ready to share my testimony. I wasn't ready to be on a platform, in a spotlight. I didn't want to share a story that I didn't have the end to.

Back when I received the promise, the second part of the prophecy that the Pastor told me is, "You're supposed to be in ministry but you're going to get in your own way!" When I heard the prophet, it made absolutely no sense to me. Ministry was nowhere on my radar and I was so broken I couldn't imagine me being healed enough to minister to someone else, at least not anytime soon. To be honest, I heard the second part of the prophecy but blocked it out my mind. This first part of the prophecy, about marriage, was in line with my plan. However, the second part of the prophecy required another level of work for me and I felt it was my turn to reap. Ministry wasn't a part of my plan and judging by the way my life was setup, it didn't seem that ministry was a part of God's plan for me either. Yet, the husband/marriage part was more logical. Therefore, that's all I zoned in on and kept with me all these years.

While I was zoning in on the husband, God was zoning in on the wife—me! I thought this prophecy was one sided and only for me to know my husband was on the way. What I learned during my process is that it was also for me to be equipped to be a wife. God started doing inward work on me. The first step was Him molding me and growing me to align with His purpose for my life. I quickly learned that my detour didn't affect God's determination to get me to my destiny.

Somewhere in between all this, I took one of the biggest faith moves of my life. I was 7 months pregnant with a two-year-old. I moved over 800 miles away to another state, minus $30,000. A job was posted within my federal agency and I applied. Long story short, although my supervisor could have offered me the job at another pay, she insisted on offering me the lower pay. The reality is I always wanted to move back south. The other part of that reality is that I always envisioned me getting the job in the south and still making the same amount of money. That was my plan.

I had applied for jobs for years. None of them landed me a job back south. After 7 years, I received the email I had been waiting on since what felt like forever. However, my soon to be boss left me in tears when she told that I had to take the $30,000 pay cut. She dug the knife even deeper telling me that if I accepted the job at this current pay she didn't know when I would be able to get a promotion. What I thought was going to be the best move of my life was starting to feel like a nightmare. I was so disappointed and mad with God. I waited 7 years for this? Really God? I had finally gotten the answer to my seven-year prayer but at a major cost—$30,000! After I prayed and weighed the pros and cons, I took a leap of faith in a situation that seemed extremely ridiculous (pregnant with a two-year-old and giving up $30,000) and decided to trust God. The crazy thing is everyone told me not to take the job and, although I didn't know the whole story, I felt in my spirit God was telling me to go! So I left the $30,000 and moved. This was the beginning of my journey into servanthood, submitting to His will as His servant. This was God's way of putting me in position to be stretched out of my comfort zone and put me back on track to destiny.

The more I had to trust Him, the closer I grew to Christ. The closer I grew to Christ, the more I sought Him and the stronger my desire to do more became. Moreover, the more I learned about Christ and witnessed His works in my own life, I started to understand the importance of sharing my journey with others. As you read in the beginning of this chapter, initially I wasn't too keen on sharing. Slowly, my own desires started to merge with the desires that Christ had for us as believers. When I would share my story, I would see how it really inspired other women and I would sometimes move women to tears. I would instantly forget about my desire to be "secretive" and "keep my business to myself" when it would come to helping another woman overcome her struggle. Slowly, I got to the point that I no longer cared if she knew that my life wasn't perfect. All I wanted her to know was that I had a journey and God brought me through. I would also make a point to give as many examples (biblical or real life) as I could to demonstrate that God is the same today, tomorrow, and forever. The more I shared my truth, the more I wanted to empower other women to be brave enough to do the same. Woman after woman, I wanted to diminish this accepted facade to look and be perfect and instead bring women closer to Christ who perfects us. Suddenly, I started to feel like I had inadvertently started a ministry.

One day during my quiet time, God told me that I needed to use my talents for His purpose. Those talents are writing and speaking. I've loved both since a child. God told me to merge my love for writing and speaking and couple that with sharing my story. One day as I was reading I started thinking about the things that I enjoy, I realized that the two things that I know for sure, besides the smiles on my children's faces whenever they see mommy, are writing and encouraging women. Just like that God told me to start a blog. Biblically Led Cornbread Fed dropped into my spirit. It was at this instance that I learned how purpose works. Unfortunately, I also learned quickly how fast fear can cripple it.

When I first heard God tell me to start the blog, I was excited and overjoyed. I started everything behind the scenes. I created a logo and had it professionally designed, I created a business plan, AND I purchased and worked on the website. I JUST DIDN'T LAUNCH THE BLOG. I started doubting my ability to truly operate in this purpose of encouraging other women because I started to reminisce on the days I could barely keep myself encouraged. Moreover, I was still harboring shame—the shame of my plan not going the way I expected it to go, which left me a single mom holding on to a promise. The funny thing is though, through the doubt and fear, I kept working. I continued to be obedient to what God had told me to do. The more I worked, the fear didn't go away, but I did it afraid. Even in the presence of the fear, there was this peace that I knew was nothing but God. He was giving me the type of peace that surpassed all understanding.

What I learned in this season was that my YES was YES to my purpose, which was ultimately the YES to begin the process to undo everything that had been done over the last seven years. It was to start the process of my healing to get me ready for the promise. As God started to reveal things to me and work on me, it made me realize I was not ready for the things I had been asking for when I was pleading to God years ago. I was carrying too much shame and emotional baggage from the past. I couldn't stand before women, I couldn't lead women, I couldn't wholeheartedly fulfill my destiny or sustain a marriage with what I was holding on to. It was at this moment that I realized I wanted a husband to fill a void. Yes, I genuinely wanted to share life with someone and wanted my children to have an awesome live-in father. Yes, I genuinely wanted my son to see an example of how man is supposed to live and be and for my daughter to have a true everyday visual of how a man is supposed to treat her, but that was the need for the husband for my children and my family. For me, the "need" was to fill the void of shame. The idea was for me to no longer have to walk around with children and no ring. It was for me to feel better about Tasha interrupting Tasha's plan. To me, the ultimate fix was simply adding the missing piece—the husband. I felt damaged and, in some crazy way, I felt that having a husband would repair me.

At first, I ignorantly thought that the YES to my blog would to automatically bring the promise.

The truth is I knew I had been avoiding my "one-on-one, don't stop until it's done, show me myself" time with God. I was afraid of the process I would have to go through to heal from past hurt, disappointments, and let downs. Don't get me wrong, I wanted to heal but I was not ready for the pruning and plucking that came along with it. It wasn't me masking imperfection because I was fine with being honest about not being perfect. It more so because I knew once it started, I could not just say, "Ok Jesus I am going to take a break on this healing process right quick, holla at me in about 2 months." Nope, I knew once I started, it started. The Bible itself said He will continue His work until it is finally finished.

Hesitantly, I STARTED my blog—the second biggest faith move of my life. Once I initiated the process, I think God took that as the green light because simultaneously He started the heart work and the issues of my heart flowed out. It was long overdue for me to stop going to great lengths to avoid the feeling of being alone with Tasha in an undistracted environment. Now that all distractions had been eliminated, to include relationships with people I entered into to fill the void, I was in solitude. It was just God and me. He had me where He wanted me years ago when He gave me the promise. It was time for us to start dealing with my true feelings: fear, anticipation, uncertainty, frustration, and disappointment. I stepped into purpose with this blog thinking that the only purpose was to help heal other women but my blog actually helped heal me. My healing began with my obedience to do what God told me to do. There were some things I had to heal from, and some things God needed to develop in me. In addition, I knew I wanted so many things in life that were dependent upon my healing and development. Not being healed would have ruined everything that I was asking God for had He given it to me immediately, to include my husband, because I wasn't prepared to be the wife.

The more I wrote blogs, the more the layers started to peel off and the more the pieces of me that I had tucked away started to rise to the top. I quickly learned that the best way for me to encourage myself and others was to do the biggest thing I was afraid to do initially... truly own my imperfections. This also meant owning the parts of me I really didn't want the world to know about or the feelings I didn't want anyone to know I felt. That's how my blog's hashtag #ImImperfectToo came about. It was my way of owning every Imperfect mistake, every Imperfect thought, and every Imperfect action to let other women know I'm just like you. Regardless of the degrees, the material possessions, the "good government job," the accolades, the things you see on social media, etc, I am imperfect. This "I'm Imperfect Too" movement was to get other women to silently say "who me" while becoming brave enough to say the phrase back. More than anything, I wanted to put an end to the façade that we had to be perfect to be purposed. In other words, still through mistakes, faults, missteps, babies out of wedlock (had to slide that in there), there was still purpose. I still have value. You still have value. Our worth has not been taken away with the bloopers of life. By 2018, I had stop running. I surrendered and begin to wholeheartedly serve Him.

With all the churches and women in ministry in Huntsville, the city started to make room for me. With all the blogs all over the world, the industry was still making room for me. Within 3 months of starting my blog I was booked for a speaking gig. I was getting new followers, likes, and comments on BLCF's Facebook daily. I was getting private messages so often from strangers about how my blog was encouraging them and calling them to action. God was sending women to me left and right to speak a word to, to the point it was bringing them to tears. Collaboration requests started springing forward. I started meeting new people like Sarah Jakes Roberts who recognized me instantly from my blog's T-Shirt I was wearing, at her Woman Evolve Conference. I was in love with who I was becoming. This blog was birthing me and showing me who I was called to be. I had peace in my spirit that I was definitely in purpose.

My blog allowed me to bring Him glory in my waiting. When I looked around me I started to notice that a lot of women were watching how I was handling my pain. Slowly, I started getting the guts to let more of me come out and reveal additional pieces of my journey. I began to get connected with more women of faith, which ultimately helped me in my own situations. Moreover, women started to tell me that my leap of faith gave them the courage to step into purpose. It became an ongoing, radical exchange of influence and faith. This new place I never wanted to be in became the place where I felt the most comfortable. I started to truly recognize the influence I had on the inside because of what I was starting to see it manifest on the outside. The biggest inspiration was seeing people that I was praying for situations change.

I felt like Jairus in some ways. You see Jairus came to Jesus, fell at His feet, and begged Jesus to come bless and heal his 12-year old daughter who was very ill. Jairus obviously had faith that Jesus could make her better. Jesus started to

The Purpose

follow Jairus to his home but He stopped to heal the woman with the issue of blood. While Jesus was performing this healing miracle, someone came to Jairus to let him know it was too late and that his daughter was dead. Jesus overheard what was said and He told Jairus, "Have no fear, just keep believing." When Jesus and Jairus made to Jairus' house, the house was filled with people who were crying because of the little girl's death. Jesus told them the girl was not dead but was sleeping. The people laughed at Him. They were sure the girl was dead. The Savior had everyone leave the house except His disciples, Jairus, and Jairus' wife. Jesus took the girl by the hand. He told her to get up. She stood up and walked.

When Jesus stopped on His way to Jairus' house to help to the woman with the issue of blood, Jesus allowed time to pass. Although Jairus probably was, Jesus was not worried about Jairus' daughter dying. He knew all along that He would heal her, even if that meant raising her from the dead. To Jairus, this could've been a moment that made him turn away from God.

Jairus was a respected, well known man of the synagogue and his daughter was laying at death's door. However, Jesus was taking His time. It was at this moment that Jairus learned that God's timing and purpose are not like ours. Sometimes He requires patience from us. Sometimes He waits longer than we think is rational. To Jairus time was of essence, just like it was for me. My desire to have a husband for my family. Jesus basically was telling Jairus, and me, I am going to meet your need but on my time. Plus, along the way I am going to demonstrate My power to perform miracles to increase your faith, like healing the woman with the issue of blood. Essentially, Jairus could then see that the same faith that he heard Jesus commend the lady with the issue of blood for having, was the same faith He needed Jairus to have for his situation—and me for my situation.

Jairus was a highly respected individual. People probably looked at him like he had it all together. That level of vulnerability that Jairus displayed going to Jesus saying now I am in need, this is where I was. The person who, from the outside looking in, looked like she had it all together was really the woman who still needed Jesus. I heard and read of the power Jesus had; however, through Him using me to help other women, I was able to truly witness it. Just as Jairus intervened on the needs of his daughter, I was sort of doing the same with my blogs and in my everyday relationships, for other women. Jesus was essentially saying keep your eyes on me, like He did Peter when Peter was walking on water (Matthew 14:22-33). Although others are saying your daughter (my promise) is dead, Jesus was telling me to focus on Him and keep believing. Believing was the key for such a pivotal time. The entire Mark chapter five was basically about Jesus healing according to faith. The woman with the issue of blood was healed and Jesus said to her in verse **34 "Daughter, your faith has made you well. Go in peace. Your suffering is over."** Jesus was illustrating to the woman with the issue of blood, to Jairus, and to me that *"your faith is what is going to do it"!*

God gave us two different, but important, perspectives here. Jesus showed us with Jairus a situation that looked dead or like a lost cause and the person, Jairus, tried Jesus first. He immediately had faith in Jesus' ability to heal his twelve-year-old daughter and went straight to the healer. Then you have the woman with the issue of blood who had this issue for twelve years. In this case Jesus showed us that even after all else has failed, still believe in Him, and He can heal you. So, whether Jesus is your first or last option, He can and will still answer your prayer when you approach with faith. Both were healed at the twelve-year stage regardless. This told me that I would still get my promise regardless of age, condition, or how long I've been afflicted. Moreover, He was no respecter of person so He doesn't prioritize one over the other. He meets you where your faith is. I had stepped out on faith with one part of the promise—ministry. Now it was time for me to revive my faith in the other part of the promise – marriage—even if it had been seven years. I had seen His power in other people's lives and I have heard of miracles happening for others. Now, I needed it for me. I was ready to declare marriage again. I was ready to truly be prepared, by God, to be a wife instead of focusing on Him sending the husband.

The Meeting Room

God has called you in for a meeting. When you received notification for the meeting, the subject line was "My Plan to Make Room for You".

Sis, get to writing...

The Purpose

Do you feel like you are operating in your purpose?

> **If no, do you know what your purpose is? Try making a list of gifts and talents that you have and pray over them.**

> **If yes, are you thriving (being obedient and fully operating) and doing exactly what God has called you to do in purpose?**

Do you have a strategy for your purpose?

If no, pray and ask God to reveal the next steps of your purpose to you.

If yes, present them back to God by praying over them and seeking His approval or modifications.

Chapter 6: The Preparation

> *1 Corinthians 2:9*
> *That is what the Scriptures mean when they say, "No eye has seen, no ear has heard, and no mind has imagined what God has prepared for those who love him."*

prep·a·ra·tion
/ˌprepəˈrāSH(ə)n/

noun

1. the action or process of making ready or being made ready for use or consideration.

2. something done to get ready for an event or undertaking.

The most important things to remember in this definition are:
1. Process.

2. Make ready.
3. Event or undertaking.

It would be times where it was extremely difficult to clap for friends who found love, those who got engaged, and those who were starting or expanding their families. I would make myself clap to not seem bitter or jealous and because, as a Christian, that's what I am supposed to do. Right? I mean, in the grand scheme of things, I was not mad because they had those things. I was just frustrated because I didn't. It was not about the person and her possessions but more about me and what I felt I lacked. More than anything, it was my dissatisfaction with me now being on the right track but still not yielding what I thought were the right results.

Even after starting this obedience process, my plan was not coming into fruition. I eagerly thought that once I stepped into purpose, the promise would start to unravel. I at least thought I would see some sign of it coming. I was ready to accept the purpose, in order to go through the process, and hopefully see the promise. No, I did not step into purpose just to get the promise, but I figured that my YES would yield the promise sooner rather than later. I felt I had already waited long enough and all God had been waiting for was my obedience to unfold it all. I didn't realize that the process in between obedience and the promise was yet another waiting period.

It was discouraging because I equated waiting with wasting. In my eyes it was a waste of time for me to wait to receive something that God had already promised me. Not to mention I had already been waiting for long enough. Waiting caused me to wonder and worry. I had moments where I would wrestle with my thoughts wondering if I heard God correctly, worried that I missed the promise, or starting to think that something was wrong. This is because the world we live in has conditioned us to want things immediately. The problem is we serve a God that sometimes requires us to wait.

In the wait, I realized a lot has to happen on the inside of us before we are ready to handle the future God has for us. As a result, God schedules a divine delay between what He promised and what He performs. This was where I was—in that divine delay. This season of singleness was vital for the groundwork of the promise and for my growth. In essence, it was a season of preparation. God was preparing me by developing and strengthening my inner character. Therefore, according to His plan, it wasn't time for the promise to come forth. It was time though for God to prepare me for His promise by developing character traits that were vital to a godly marriage.

God was nudging me out of my comfort zone toward unfamiliar experiences that would encourage me to rely on and trust Him. Before I could move forward into this new thing, I had let go of some things that had been with me. This meant trusting and believing what I couldn't see when my flesh was yearning for what I was leaving. Initially, I tried to hold on to what was familiar before I had the confidence that the new thing was right for me. I was holding one foot firmly where I was while the other foot was attempting to stretch towards someplace new. Eventually I lost my footing and fell over. God wants us to trust Him by doing what He wants us to do and going where He wants us to go. We must learn to let go of what we have before we take hold of something new. In this time, we rely on God to meet all our needs—including my "need" for a husband.

Through these unfamiliar experiences, I started to notice that even with me stepping into purpose, beginning to heal, and relinquishing control to God, I was still holding on to the shame of being a single mom. I realize that most of it was because a piece of me was still subconsciously holding on to my plan of how my life was supposed to look. There was no way I could have truly surrendered and truly had faith that God was going to work it out if I was STILL holding onto shame. There still had to be some unbelief there that my situation was truly going to change. There were still pieces of me that did not have the proper faith and other parts that were not truly content with my current life.

The more I accepted what God was doing, the easier it was to release myself from who I had been, to embrace who He was calling me to be. God stripped me of what I thought needed to happen so I could see what He was already doing. I stopped fighting Him to make it what I wanted it to be and let Him make it what He wanted it to be. In that moment, I was single so that meant being content in my singleness. This also entailed me fighting pass those difficult and frustrating moments when I became dissatisfied with my single relationship status. I had to push pass the unfulfilled desire to be loved by a man and instead love every piece of me. That season of singleness was unique and filled with both challenges and opportunities. The first challenge, which could also be seen as an opportunity, was contentment.

We usually don't learn contentment until we give up seeking our own way. I had lived a discontented life for so long that I finally felt the shift of only wanting what God wanted me to have. I was tired of miserably waiting and now wanted peace in my wait. I found peace in getting to know Tasha again. In the past she had changed so much, as a result of the pain, and she was now becoming a different person for the purpose. I allowed myself to stop being numb and started to humble myself. There is a difference. Numb would be defined as unable to feel anything. Although I was numb to the situation, I still felt every piece of the pain from my past, every ounce. So, the first step was to making the decision to stop pretending like I wasn't hurting. In order to do that I had to humble myself. God honors us when we are humble, in part, because we are open to His guidance. It's only then that He can show us what is right and teach us in His way **(Psalm 25:9)**. I humbled myself by acknowledging my need for Him to rebuild me in a healthy way. Biblically Led Cornbread Fed had started the work but the wounds were deeper than just admitting there was an issue. I started with repentance then prayer. This gave God access to every wound, not just the wounds I presented to Him. I needed to find the wounds that were so deep that they were still bleeding out to the nursed parts of me. It was at this moment that I realized—yes, I needed God and prayer but—I needed something even beyond that. So, I started going to therapy.

The Preparation

I used to be one that thought therapy was for those who were crazy or had a true mental illness. I never thought of needing to heal as a reason to go to therapy. I am so glad that a friend introduced me to her therapist because therapy allowed me to go back and rehash the details of traumatic events in a healthy way. I rehashed that moment when the reality first set in that the relationship would not work out and I would be a single mother. I recalled when I **DROWNED**, like drowned to the point I didn't want a life jacket, a boat, or even a float. I didn't even want the Lifeguard – God – to come for me. The only lifeline I was willing to accept was the father being ready to do this family thing! I wallowed in it, complaining to my friends, because I never imagined this to be my life. I wanted to throw the whole experience away. Since I couldn't, I tucked it away!

I let that situation win because I didn't accept God's full armor to properly engage in battle. As a result, I developed a daily coping mechanism of **"mind-over-matter".** I pretended like the situation had no affect over me. Yet, every time

I had to go to parents' night out alone, every year there was a "Donuts with Dad", or when I needed a mental break, the reality would slap me in the face. Ultimately, it caught up with me and when it did, it sent me back into an emotional whirlwind! I wanted to throw the whole experience away. Since I couldn't, I tucked it away!

During that crucial time, instead of acknowledging God is in control and seeking Him, I tried to manufacture my own peace. I created my own picture-perfect existence by only focusing on the good parts of life – family, friends, career, material possessions, and predominantly, being a mom! I coped by creating the life I desired, hoped for, or imagined in the areas I COULD control. I wasn't hiding my life. I just wasn't tackling it in the hopes of healing from the disappointment. I pulled the breaker in the heart-valve switch to the pain. For years, I managed by numbing myself.

Fast forward years later, I was ready to come to terms with my truth in a way that didn't make me feel defeated. Even though my plan didn't work and that left me in pain, there was still a promise waiting to be fulfilled. I will never forget, about three sessions in, my therapist looked me directly in the eyes with the sternest look ever and said, "This is your wife training." The most interesting thing about this is I started going to therapy because of a work-related issue. I talked about it in my blog "I Gave God a $30,000 Offering Part 2." My supervisor and I were having strife because she had been promising me a promotion that she never delivered. Every time it was time to deliver what she promised, she would come with a new set of criteria for me to get the promotion. While talking about my frustration with a friend she recommended her therapist. I never intended on talking about anything other than my job, my feelings about my job, and my supervisor. My therapist let me get away with that in the first two sessions. In this third session, she asked me, "If your job made everything spill over, what made everything boil to the top?" In that moment, the true preparation started. So much healing happened in that room because of that one question. Biblically Led Cornbread Fed was birthed here too because so much that was released gave me the courage to finally push publish. Still to this day, I think about her comment of it being my "wife training" and smirk because I truly believe God used her to remind me that the promise wasn't dead. He was notifying me of the preparation ahead.

In some ways I felt like Simeon in the Bible. Luke Chapter 2:25-28, it talks about a man named Simeon who was righteous and devout and was eagerly waiting for the Messiah to come and rescue Israel. The Holy Spirit revealed to him that he would not die until he had seen the Lord's Messiah. That day the Spirit led him to the Temple. So, when Mary and Joseph came to present baby Jesus to the Lord as the law required, Simeon was there. He took the child in his arms and praised God.

Although we don't know much about Simeon, we know that he was righteous, devout, and filled with the Holy Spirit. I would consider myself to be of pretty good character and reputation, like Simeon, and like him also waiting on God. I never understood, until now, why "good people" didn't get their prayers answered right away. I understand more now that it is not because we have done something wrong or we are not worthy. It's due to the preparation that goes into getting an answered prayer, both in us and in the process. For both me and Simeon, there was a divine pause between God speaking and God showing. Although God had delivered both of us a promise, it seemed to be an intermission between God declaring and God doing. The preparation allowed me to develop a Simeon spirit. See Simeon kept worshipping, kept praying, kept giving God thanks, and kept being faithful during the wait because he understood that him waiting didn't mean that God was no longer worthy of all those things. We have to be careful not to allow the waiting/preparation period, the divine delay, or the intermission to taint how we see God. He is still the God who is omnipotence, omniscience, and omnipresence.

The preparation taught me when you are following the plan that God has designed for your life, your purpose is revealed and things start to unfold. My roadmap included several wrong turns and countless red lights, which taught me to appreciate the detours in life. It also renewed my faith in His promise, developed my trust in God's plan, and taught me to wait in expectancy again. The truth is, over the seven years, I was praying for the promise with more faith that it wouldn't happen than I did that He would do it. My next level required me to stop diluting my prayers requests with fear, doubt, and insecurity. The next level had everything to do with me diluting everything down to belief. Spending years being double minded and unstable (James 1:8), I did not have room for anything other than belief and this divine interruption was the best time to be conditioned and prepared.

Over time I started waiting properly because I believed that God was going to do what He spoke. I started waiting properly because I believed that God was going to do what He declared. I decided to use my waiting as an expression to God of my faith. I stopped looking for external confirmations and validation because I had already had a prophet speak the promise and, like Simeon, the Holy Spirit had already spoken to me as well. I started having enough faith in God to take Him at His word regardless of what it looked like. For once, I was rejoicing for God's interruption. It was an unexpected but joyful interruption that allowed me to prepare for the promise. This was better than getting the promise and losing it because I didn't have the character traits, faith, and spiritual discipline to keep it. I reminded myself countless times that when I am waiting God is working and I have to allow God time to finish His work. Moreover, I started to truly believe that whatever He had me waiting for was worth the wait.

The Training Room

Let's examine your spiritual endurance. Before God gives us what He promised, He has to be sure we are prepared for the spiritual warfare that comes with it. No situation is perfect nor did God promise us no more tests once we get to the next level. The difference is that now we have to go into battles with God. Without Him we have the potential to go astray or, even worse, lose the battle. Whether it is a job, a marriage, becoming a mother, stepping into purpose, whatever, God has the VICTORY plan and we want to come out VICTORIOUS!

Sis, get to writing...

The Preparation

Is there a divine delay happening right now in your life?

How are you waiting? Do you honestly feel you are waiting properly? Why?

Is there something that you have diluted your prayer request for because you are too afraid to believe in again?

Chapter 7: The Perfection

> *James 1:4*
> *So, let it grow, for when your endurance is fully developed, you will be perfect and complete, needing nothing.*

per·fec·tion
/pərˈfekSH(ə)n/

noun

1. the condition, state, or quality of being free or as free as possible from all flaws or defects.
2. the action or process of improving something until it is faultless or as faultless as possible.

The most important things to remember in this definition are:
   1. *Free.*
   2. *Improving.*

The preparation period had me looking at obedience in an entirely different light. The most important thing about Simeon's story is that he was obedient and moved when God told him to move. Had he not heeded to God's instructions he could have missed the opportunity to see the promise fulfilled. God never forgets or fails on His promises but it is up to us to remain faithful and trust in His words. After years of trying to get to the promise, I learned that the difference in making it to the promise like Simeon and roaming like an Israelite is faith and obedience. Like the Israelites, I had sacrificed for years by praying, fasting, and doing my duties but my obedience is what was going to allow me to see "Israel's redemption/salvation."

Operating in purpose and in preparation to get to the promise God's way, Tasha changed so much. The work God did on the inside of me changed my feelings and outlook towards almost everything going on in my life, to include my outlook on myself. God started taking me to different levels and into different areas that I didn't think I was prepared or qualified for. In spite of this, since I knew it was God, I complied in obedience. Likewise, some things that I wanted and expected changed because I was constantly changing and I desired something different. I had some seeds in my "heart of control" that God uprooted. In replacement, He planted some seeds of surrender and submission. The heart that was once shut down was now revived and functioning to its full capacity all because I let God in. In addition, during this critical time, I had to carefully watch what seeds I allowed to take root in my transformed heart.

The number one situation that my new heart helped with was the relationship with the first man who left me, my father. During this seven-year-journey, I forgave the first man who left me with a wound that I didn't even realize was bleeding. I forgave my biological father Easter 2019, for being absent from my life for 33 years. Let me give you the back story.

My father has always had an open invitation to be a part of my life. He just chose not to be 100%

present. I've always known who he was and he has always chosen to be inactive. On the rare occasions we did make contact, the conversations were cold and felt forced. By the time I hit adolescence, I accepted the fact that we would not have a relationship and I had no interest in trying to salvage it. I no longer tried to mend that relationship or work on one with him. He was not present for my firsts, my graduations, my big moments, the birth of my children, anything.

In 2017, my paternal oldest sister got married and at her wedding began the mending process for my biological father and me. The wedding weekend, he expressed wanting a relationship with me, and we all—him, my paternal siblings, and me—met up for lunch and had a great time with each other. Fast forward two years, Easter 2019, I met up with this same sister in MS. While there, my father's wife apologized for her role in the process of my father being inactive. She also apologized for fostering an environment where she did not accept the children that were not hers. My father's mother also apologized for the same. It felt like things were mending perfectly, 32 years later.

In June 2019, I went to visit my father for the first time since we had mended our relationship. Everything felt natural and normal. This time I took my children over with me. In case I didn't mention it before, I had been avoiding bringing my children into the mix because of a few things. Number one, I was trying to process it all myself and figure out how I would adjust. Number two, I wanted to be sure my father was serious about being an active father and grandfather before I altered my children's life with the news that this new man was mom's dad. They were already accustomed to identifying the man that helped my mom raise me as granddad. So to open this can of worms would probably also open up a lot of questions that I did not want to address if this was not going to be a permanent change. Therefore, I had been putting off this part until I felt like it was absolutely necessary.

It became necessary during this visit. The main reason was because my father attempted to interact with my children and they were pretty hesitant. I know it was mainly due to the fact that I had not thoroughly expressed to them who they were interacting with. They knew it was safe because mom was there and I allowed it but nothing was really put into context. Also, my father kept referencing himself as my dad and "paw paw" so I wanted to also clear up anything that my "intelligent, hear everything children" may have been confused about. On the three-hour drive back home, I mustered up enough courage to explain to my children that the man who was hugging and talking to them was my dad. I told them I had two dads which meant they had two grandads. I asked if they had any questions and they told me no with a smile. It was as if God had already gone before me, explained it all, and made everything ok. I was so relieved. I asked them what they did think they wanted to call him since they already called one grandad. They said "paw paw" and we went with it.

I now see that it is so true that everything happens in God's order because, had my father attempted to connect with the Tasha who was still dealing with broken pieces of herself from past hurts and past relationships, I am not sure I would have been as open. However, a part of the preparation was me learning to carry out the principles of Christ to truly forgive and extend grace. Moreover, my own struggles made me realize that there are no perfect people. Also, just like I want to be a recipient of God's grace, I offered the same to my father. So, I give much credit to spiritual maturity during the preparation period that I was able to approach the situation with love when we did reconnect. Taking this approach allowed me to operate in forgiveness when faced with the situation 30 plus years later. When he and I initially started to form a relationship, I thought all was forgiven and well. Yet, shortly after, I realized that in order for me to let my guard down I needed to have a true heart to heart talk with my father. It was not to stay stuck in the past but to make peace for the future.

One day on the way to therapy, I called my father and had the honest conversation with him I have wanted to have with him for years. I was heading to Healed Avenue and I had a few stops to make along the way. So that meant I also had to address any speed bumps or detours that would possibly stop me from making it to my healed destination. I told my father I loved the fact that years later he was being very intentional about having a relationship with me and that Easter weekend was an awesome start. I informed him that something still felt off in my spirit that I couldn't put my finger on until now. I explained that while his wife and mom apologized and we all had a great time Easter weekend, the person who did not take ownership of his responsibility in the situation was him. I was honest with him about wanting an apology for him choosing to not be involved and not being an active father. I made it clear that I was not doing this to make him feel horrible or to stay stuck in the past but so that we could properly move forward in healthy way. The biggest thing I opened up to him about was that I was now in the situation but as the parent instead of the child. Being in the situation from a parent perspective was making me oddly relive the story of my father, which was making it a tough situation for me to move forward from without his apology. He apologized and admitted that he ultimately chose not to be present because of his own selfish reasons and dealing with his own issues. It finally sunk in that his absence had nothing to do with me.

God continued to confirm this for me. I attended the Sarah Jakes Roberts' Woman Evolve Conference and there was a session titled, "Daddy Issues". According to the program, the purpose of the session was to minister on what was, for some us, our very first heartbreak. Describing it this way, I made the essential connection that a heartbreak from a dad can fundamentally be registered as a heartbreak from a man. So, this relationship could possibly lay the foundation for the relationship with the man that God has for me. I was happy that I was able to confront this daddy issue before it became a marital issue for me. This year was the first year that I was genuinely able to celebrate Father's Day. Before now, Father's Day was always the day that I sat aside to acknowledge other great fathers that were connected to me. However, 2019 was the first time in 33 years I said "Happy Father's Day Dad" to my biological father.

The date August 2, 2019 was so unforgettable as I experienced another first with my dad. It was a weekend that I intentionally took a trip to spend time with my dad, his family, and my paternal siblings. Unlike before when this trip was solely for my mom's side of the family, everything finally felt complete. After 33 years, I finally was able to see and spend time with both sides of my families. I was going to visit my dad. Hearing the word dad come out of my mouth sounded so weird but I love how it felt.

While I was there, I also spent time with a guy that I met a month prior. For the first time it felt like I was dating from a healed place. It didn't feel as if I was lacking something and looking for a guy to fill it. I felt whole. I was only seeking from him what I wanted—the love and companionship of a man—and not a man to fill the place that my father didn't. I now had my father to fill that role so I wasn't projecting those expectations off on another man. It was a feeling that I cannot explain. I know this entire time I have been going through the process of healing and preparing for this moment but on Sunday, August 11, 2019, I actually felt it. It was the best feeling in the world.

Through all of this, I continued going to therapy to work on reprogramming myself to get rid of old habits, thoughts, and behaviors. It was also during this time that I realized my role in it all. There was no misunderstanding that I played a major role by not letting go of toxic relationships and/or going back after certain encounters. However, I went a step deeper. I took responsibility for not being transparent or intentional about what I wanted. I realized that then I didn't really know what I wanted but I knew what I didn't want. I didn't want to be alone forever. Nevertheless, I didn't know how to make it not happen. No, I was not a dorm mat or just letting a man do or treat me any kind of way. However I didn't relay the proper standards, expectations, and qualities. The truth is I was hoping that the man had the proper instructions and could show me the way. Each time I was basically getting in a car and not giving the driver directions. Then I was getting upset when I made it to the final destination. For years, I made it to unknown destinations and got upset. Even worse, sometimes I would let the driver pass my stop and not say anything, while hoping to get back on the correct route.

So, the one chance I had to finally make steps to correcting this behavior was when I reconnected with my father. I had to explain to him how he hurt me and how I expected to move forward. The more I held off, the more I felt like I was in previous situations with other men where I would move forward and "forget what he had done." I felt like I was in one of my past relationships where I allowed a man back into my life without us truly processing the issue and the pain or without me truly expressing how he made me feel. For the first time, a man apologized to me followed by truly changed behavior. For the first time, I truly forgave a man that hurt me without recounting the incident. I learned true forgiveness that day I talked to my dad. Forgiveness helped heal the last little part of me.

This reminded me of Joseph in the Bible. Joseph's brothers sold him into slavery and later came to Joseph for resources. Joseph forgave them when he had the authority to show unforgiveness. Earlier, when Joseph's brothers had sold him into slavery, perhaps he had been very angry with them. Maybe he wanted their punishment to be them being torn away from their families and sold as slaves too. What if Joseph felt the way most of us often feel when we are hurt and want the other person to hurt the way that they hurt us? Although we do not know exactly how Joseph felt, what we do know is that the end result was what God asks all of us to do—forgiveness! When Joseph reunited with them 20 years later, Joseph was free and was governor in charge of all the land and all the food. His family did not recognize him because he'd grown up and was wearing different clothes. Not only did Joseph change physically, he had grown spiritually as result of God's perfection. Joseph had forgiven his brothers for selling him into slavery and he was happy to see them again. Joseph said to his brothers "I am Joseph, your brother" and they were amazed and worried. They were worried that Joseph would be angry with them and put them in jail or kill them. Although I wasn't going to jail or kill my father, I can only imagine that my dad felt the same way, worried that I would reject him. Actually, my dad has told me several times that he didn't think I would accept him and love him. However, like Joseph, I said, "I forgive you." In both cases, mine and Joseph's, the entire family was together again. Instead of exercising the option to show resentment, I forgave and allowed my actions to show it like Joseph.

Likewise, I exerted this same level of forgiveness to ALL the men of my past. I no longer cared about the day that they would receive vengeance for the pain that they caused. Honestly, I really was no longer concerned about the pain that they had caused. I was only focused on healing from that pain and I was ready to move forward and love in a healthy way. Now, it was all starting to make sense, what my therapist said about this being my wife training. I had to let go of my plan, sort through the pain, and receive the promise that revived my faith and helped change my perspective. This all put me in a position to obediently start to operate in purpose, while being prepared and perfected for my promotion! The promotion was not in the title of "wife" but in the type of woman I was able to be due to me being healed and whole. This ultimately led to me truthfully being wife material. Before, I only wanted the promise but I didn't want the process. Yet, the process was the only way to get to the Promised Land.

My wife training taught me to value the journey over the destination. When God told me I was going to be a wife I was like yes sign me up. If someone had told me that in the process, I was going to lose myself, be a single mom, and endure so much, I would've said remove my name from the roster. It was clearly all God because LaTasha would not have chosen this route. The issue with that is I needed to go through it all to get to the promise. It did not have to be all pain but the pain was a part of my journey because of me taking pieces of my process and putting it into my hands. Even with that, I love that He is such a loving God that He still got me to my destination—despite my self-imposed detour. The process is what I needed to sustain the promise. Going through the process is what earned me my promotion.

The Operating Room

Remember earlier in the book, you scheduled a doctor's appointment for your pain. Well, the doctor scheduled you for an operation. It is an issue that has to be corrected internally first before it can become better on the outside. The day has come and it is now time for you to go into surgery so He can assess and repair the damage.

Sis, get to writing…

Is there anyone that you need to forgive?

You know women with absent fathers are not the only ones who can have a daddy issue, right? How is your relationship with your dad sis?

The Perfection

Are you verbalizing or ready to verbalize how to be loved properly in relationships?

Is there any other pain left in you that you have not addressed at this point?

The Seven Year Promise

Chapter 8: The Promotion

> *Psalm 75:6-7*
> *For exaltation*
> *(promotion) comes neither from the east*
> *nor from the west nor from the south.*
> *But God is the Judge...*

pro·mo·tion
/prəˈmōSH(ə)n/

noun

the action of raising someone to a higher position or rank or the fact of being so raised.

The most important things to remember in this definition are:
1. *Higher position.*
2. *Raised.*

God's plan for us seems crazy and, most of all, impossible sometimes. Sometimes we get wrapped up in questions like "how could this be?" or "will this ever by?". I was in between these two questions. I was at a point that I was healed, I was passing tests, in purpose, and on the right path with God but I was also single as a dollar bill. Even at this point, when I would date, I would become frustrated eventually. I became frustrated by the lack of consistency. I also became frustrated because I just couldn't seem to sync with anyone that shared my same goals and values. None of the guys seem to be up to my speed spiritually, mentally, emotionally, and/or stability. Unlike before though, when I would recognize this, I ended it immediately. Gone were the days of sitting around hoping and looking for the potential I thought the guy exuded. Moreover, I started to see a lot of men through their baggage—the pain they wouldn't unpack or put down—and I made the decision not to let it be projected on me. I was no longer into playing nurse or dressing wounds.

My newfound vision and priorities changed my core values that I desired in my husband. During this time, I learned so much about myself. For the first time in 30 plus years, I wrote a "What I desire in a mate" list. I also made a list of non-negotiables and deal breakers. I now understood why it would be hard to achieve relationship goals while wounded from past hurt. Moreover, I understood that it was also hard to achieve relationship goals with no goals of what the mate should be. Before moving forward, I decided to go back to who I used to be, the person who was excited for the Promise. I wanted to do my part to finish what God started, His way.

I was more content in my single status than I had ever been. I was dating myself, putting myself first, and loving LaTasha more than I ever had. I was more focused on who I could be, to and for me, than I was to and for a man. Every change I made was for me. Every choice I made was for me. Every piece of me that I altered was for me. None of it was with "preparing to be his wife" in mind. Did I still think about my husband? Yes!

However, it didn't drive my decisions because everything was done in consultation and partnership with God. Therefore, I knew that at the right time, He would bring the right man that would appreciate the pruning and plucking. That right man would fit every change, choice, alteration, and decision. That right man would fit ME... ***the healed and whole me***!

I was still going to therapy, I was walking in my calling, and I was enjoying where I was currently, without wishing towards the future. I started to realize the joy in not being married and the opportunity that it brought me. Although I had my children, they were my only responsibility outside of myself. I didn't have to consult with anyone about what I wanted to do and I had all the time in the world—outside of work and my children. I could use my free time to completely work on my blog and other purposeful projects. I made the choice to be more intentional about using this time wisely rather than using this time hoping. I was maximizing my current season. I was still on a journey of saying yes to things that scared me and stretched me out of my comfort zone. Most importantly, I was saying yes to God and myself. I had a sense of peace that while I was busying saying yes to God, God was busy orchestrating some things in the background. I was working on being content on my current level but I felt in my spirit God was already working on my elevation.

I was in MS for a funeral and, while there, one of my closest cousins invited me to a cookout. Later, we left the cookout and all hung out. I was walking through the crowd and someone grabbed my arm. I turned around and a voice said "I let you walk pass me at the cookout but I am not going to allow that now." I turned to see such a handsome, chocolate man with the prettiest white teeth. He was smiling so bright and so was I at this point because I was smitten.

The rest of the night he was super protective of me. He interfered when two guys attempted to approach and insisted that I put his number in my phone and let him see for proof. He even walked my cousin and me to the car because he said "every time he let me out of his sight it seemed someone was trying to interfere." We walked hand-in-hand to the car while talking and flirting. Totally different than what I usually do but yet it felt so natural.

I was so shocked at the way he pursued me and his level of persistence. This felt like the old school way I saw it done in the movies but I had never truly experienced in my adult life. I was witnessing how I've heard it should be, from a biblical standpoint. If I had to truly describe it, it was sort of the way a man would act when he just knows something is different about a woman so he makes sure he purses her correctly. Here I was seven years later being pursued correctly and it felt great. I would like to accredit most of this from me oozing vibes of the new healed and whole me.

Everything seemed to be going well. We were getting to know each other, moving at a great pace, and making some plans for a possible future. I went before God seeking another piece of the promise. Instead of giving me the answer right away, God threw me a test. It had been so long since I faced a true test in the area of dating/relationships. Nonetheless, with me being so content in my singleness, I thought I would be ready to pass these tests I used to fail. See, it is easy to be full of faith and at peace when you see signs that look like what God revealed. However, fear crept in as soon as things started going in a different direction than what I expected. Honestly, initially, I started to worry and question. I was literally in the middle of complaining to a friend when I stopped myself mid-sentence. I said, "I sound like the woman I was when I initially received the promise and before my faith and relationship with God were strengthen." In that moment, I was acting like the Israelite who was wandering around the mountain NOT the one who is about to enter into the Promised Land. I felt like I had been thrown back into the wilderness but what I soon realized was that I was still in position. Even though what was going on around me started to look wacky, I still didn't feel pushed back from the promise. I felt I was still right where I needed to be. In prior situations, I was working outside of God's will so I immediately started to count myself out when things went in the direction of what I thought was astray.

Remembering that, I immediately started to put everything I learned over these last seven years into practice, from the prayer to the techniques I learned in therapy.

I wanted to do like the children of Israel and send spies into the land. See, the old LaTasha would be picking up the phone calling a psychic by now. Yep, your girl went through a brief period where I used to blow up the phone lines trying to get a glimpse into my future, especially after receiving the prophecy. Since God gave me the end but no middle, I was relying on the psychic to give me what God did not—the step by step play. It was such a horrible point in my life because it only added more confusion. I was looking for an external force to confirm what God said. I couldn't have insulted God more and I certainly didn't want to do it again. I knew I had come too far. I refused to push myself back into confusion or further away from the promise. I knew and could feel in my spirit I was too close to jump back into "planning" mode. Similarly, the Israelites were right on the doorstep of the promise when the spies went out to view the

Promised Land. The spies came back with a negative report, which changed the Israelites' attitude. The Israelites then started to question why God brought them from where they were and never talked positive about where they were going. In this moment, I used this as an example of what not to do. Been there done that. I was ready to operate differently. Therefore, I sought another resource that I did not have before—my dad!

Initially, I would have rather stayed stagnant than cross over to this new me. I wasn't ready to be vulnerable and transparent. I wasn't ready to put my pride to the side and admit how I felt. The oxymoron is I was saying I was ready for the promise though. Immediately, I had to remember the woman I became when I wandering like an Israelite. I wasn't going to be defeated easily like I was in the past and I wasn't going to let the old LaTasha start to spring back up. The old LaTasha wanted to resort to petty tactics when she felt her back was against the wall. The old LaTasha had the urge to run from the conversation. The new LaTasha heard her therapist voice in her head saying, "When you start wanting to play games and thinking of reverting back to unhealthy behaviors, do the opposite of what you were thinking of doing." The new LaTasha made the intentional choice to heed to what I learned in my "wife training" aka therapy. LaTasha was so far out that she could not go back to that wandering woman. It was time for me to keep going to who I was called to be. The conversation I mentioned in "The Perfection" chapter, that I had with my dad, set the tone for my communication with men going forward. Being able to be vulnerable with my dad about my relationship with him gave me the freedom to be vulnerable with him about my relationships with other men. For the first time ever in my life, I picked up the phone and called my dad to get his advice. I explained to him what was going on and he gave me advice that I am sure saved me from wandering again.

God revealed another piece of the promise to me right before He threw a wrench in the plans. If you know what a wrench is then you know that a wrench applies torque to turn objects by either loosening or fastening items, like nuts and bolts. The amazing thing about a wrench is that it has one fixed jaw point at the top of the wrench and one moveable jaw, which can be tightened against something to provide grip for turning. In the same way, God was the "fixed jaw point at the top" and I was the "moveable jaw". As God was loosening some things and tightening others, my thoughts were similar to that of the Israelites when they asked God if He brought them there to torture them. ***Exodus 14:11 says and they said to Moses, "Why did you bring us out here to die in the wilderness? Weren't there enough graves for us in Egypt? What have you done to us? Why did you make us leave Egypt?*** Could I have not been left alone in my singleness? Could I just have not met this guy and instead continue to deal with my vulnerability and transparency issues alone? I quickly realized I wasn't as ready as I thought but later found out that I was prepared. God was saying the same thing to me that He said to Moses, ***"Then the Lord said to Moses, "Why are you crying out to me? Tell the people to get moving!"*** So, I kept moving!

LaTasha kept moving, which meant not going back to the old me but continuing in my new ways. This meant me moving forward in my new mentality of no longer falling in love with a man's potential. This guy seemed right. He approached me correctly but he was inconsistent, among other things. The old me was ready to make excuses for him and list out the reasons I should probably stay to see how it would turn out. The new me was ready to give reasons why I should go. I listened to my heart, and my dad, and peacefully walked away. The most important revelation was that when I walked away, I walked away still having radical faith that the promise was coming soon. This encounter substantiated my growth for me because it didn't alter or make me adjust my faith. Moreover, it didn't distract me from staying the course. That's what it means to follow God—to open your life to the unexpected Christ. It means encountering Him in the ordinary and finding that life has become extraordinary. I was ready to witness the impossible become possible. I discerned that the key was believing differently. I literally got down on my knees and asked God to help any unbelief. I was letting God know that I believed Him and I still believed in His promise. I had to trust that my belief would break the curse too. I was ready to war differently. I was ready to go toe to toe with whatever was trying to steal my growth or my promise. Everything that I learned in the last seven chapters was my weapon. I walked boldly into battle because I knew I was walking in obedience; therefore, I knew God was going to cover me.

I got to the root of it all and realized that there was still some fear present but this fear was a different fear. It was the fear of everything actually working out. I had this crazy urge to create chaos in the absence of it. Similar to the Israelites, because of this, God couldn't take me into the free land that was promised just yet since my mind wasn't 100% free. Sometimes God leads us the hard way instead of the easy way for this very reason. It is so we can learn to lean on Him. An example would be when God led the children of Israel the long, difficult way through the wilderness to prepare them for the battles they would face in possessing the Promised Land. **Exodus 13:17-18** says ***"When Pharaoh finally let the people go, God did not lead them along the main road that runs through Philistine territory, even though that was the shortest route to the Promised Land. God said, "If the people are faced with a battle, they might change their minds and return to Egypt.""*** So, basically God led them in a roundabout way through the wilderness toward the Red Sea. Thus, the Israelites left Egypt like an army ready for battle. From the text it is understood that the wilderness was required. It was the Israelites journey to becoming free. This too was my journey to freedom, which required a painful process of leaving what was familiar and stepping out to see that there was something better for me. It also required me to stop getting in my own way. Side note, although the Israelites (and I) had to go through the wilderness, I wonder if the time was really required (40 years for the Israelites and seven for me). I don't know that answer for sure but what I do know for sure is I didn't want to add any more time. The best way not to add more time was to let God do a thorough work in me so that I could leave my "wilderness" behind and enter into my Promised Land.

Like the Israelites, God was supplying me with manna. If you know anything about the manna that God gave to the Israelites, it was only good for the DAY. The manna literally could not be sustained for the next day (Exodus 16:19). It could not be stored because it was truly the word, nourishment, and fuel for that day. God started revealing more pieces to the promise and giving me more steps for the day. It was enough to increase my faith and know that He was working but it was not sustainable enough for me to independently wander away. I still had a dependency on Him because I did not have all the answers and could not go ahead to handle the rest myself. This was a total mindset shift from the "The Plan" chapter. During "The Plan" era, all I needed was a few crumbs to fuel me to move forward with what I wanted. Now, in "The Promise" era, those crumbs were used to feed my faith in His Plan. God was revealing things as He could trust me with them, based on my level of faith and spiritual maturity. It took Him seven years to reveal the next piece of the promise to me and the reason is clear. It is because in those 7 years I had to get the promise, shift my perspective, step into purpose, get prepared, and let God perfect me.

God's perfection didn't feel good but it looked good when it was all over. After my perfecting, I felt like Mary. God gave us both a promise of birthing some new—me a marriage and Mary a promise of birthing Jesus. Mary's journey on the way to give birth was similar to mine on the way to the promotion—a tough one. I can honestly say that I am so glad God did not give me my husband while I was "on my way to Bethlehem". Had my husband walked in on the transformation I am sure it would not have been as appealing as it is today, just as Mary wasn't when she was pregnant and trudging towards the promise. The awesome thing is, when you see a figurine of Mary, she looks nothing like she had completed a 100-mile journey while pregnant. She doesn't look like she had been turned away from an actual room (Luke 2:7) or as if she had spent hours in painful labor. It seemed as if there was no blood, no dirt, no sweat, and no stench. It was as if she didn't even give birth in a barn. I came out of my "birthing process" just the way Mary did, with no blemishes from what I had been through. When my transformation was complete, I came out blemish free and with a glow. I came out loving myself enough this time around that I am truly ready to love someone else. I am now ready to love them in a way that allows me to add to myself, not lose myself. I am ready for someone to complement me, not complete me, because I am self-sustaining. I am not perfect but I am whole. I am a whole woman seeking a whole, not perfect, man to go along with me on my journey. In the midst, hopefully we become better together than we were apart. In the words of Bishop T.D. Jakes, "A whole man plus a whole woman together equals a whole marriage."

I told you in the pain chapter that I felt like Job

in the Bible. I felt like I was going through a cycle of events to be tortured and did not understand why it was happening. I felt I had everything stripped away from me. Well, if you know how the story of Job ends, this is where I am now. My latter days are blessed way more than my former. ***Job Chapter 42:12 So the LORD blessed Job in the second half of his life even more than in the beginning.*** I now understand that this journey and this book was never about me being a wife but becoming a wife. I had to grow into the person who was ready to manifest the promise. From the instant the enemy attacked me, God had my restoration in mind. All those years I was so focused on changing my last name and being attached to him (my husband) when God wanted to change my spirit and attach me to Him (my God). Being anchored in Him allows me to be ready for him and I now understand why the Bible says ***"Seek first the kingdom of God and all else will be added to you" (Matthew 6:33).*** For the last two years I have been intentional about seeking the Kingdom and, in doing that, so much has been added to me. I am still baffled at how it all ended for my good and how ecstatic I am with the results. I stand now a wife ready to love like I have never been hurt and I am prepared for "all else" to be added to me. Unlike before, my self-image can't be distorted based on what the devil tries to throw in my face because I have an unshakeable inner confidence based on what God says about me. Even on days where my situation seems to be unchanged and not moving, I remind myself that all promotion comes from God. Therefore, if He promoted me that means I am still in position and I am still qualified. As a matter of a fact, I might have to write a sequel because God blew my mind with what He revealed right before I finished writing this book. It is definitely a sign that in these seven years He was working while I was waiting, in an unexpected—yet blissful—way!

2 Corinthians 4:8-9
We are pressed on every side by troubles,
but we are not crushed.
We are perplexed,
but not driven to despair.

The Board Room

Guess what? The job you have wanted for years has now been posted and it is time for you to apply. You have made sure you have all the qualifications and your resume is ready and up-to-date. The most important thing to remember is to take everything that you have learned, along the way, with you. Get ready to use the wisdom and strategy from Him.

Sis, get to writing...

What are you going to do when you get the call for the job (whatever it is that you are asking God for)?

What does an abundant life look like to you?

The Promotion

Write a letter to the woman you want to become in this new position.

LaTasha's Room

I reached out to my prayer partner on September 8, 2019. We went back and forth about me being finished with the book. She applauded me for my obedience in writing the book. She was there from the beginning when I initially said "I don't want to do this God." She was there for the middle when I started on the book and said to myself, "I will write every chapter but the last chapter titled "The Promotion" because that has to be the chapter that is completed once I am at least engaged." She was there for the end when God threw a wrench in the plans and I still didn't stop being obedient, through the disappointment and confusion. She sent me a voice memo that said,

"Tasha, what got me girl is you're finishing the book in the ninth month like you're giving birth. You're a mother so you know in the ninth month the woman gives birth and [she stops and says I am getting emotional and

about to cry] I'm just thinking about everything you've been through and now you finally get to give birth to your baby. As you give birth to this book, you're giving birth to the promise because of your obedience. So I am so excited for you Tasha that you have been obedient, that you didn't let the setback or the confusion make you say ok God you know what I am done writing the book because in the process of writing the book I thought this was going to happen but you threw a wrench and I am confused. So, I am so proud of you that you continued to preserve and you didn't let what human beings did stop you from doing what God told you to do. Love you!"

I immediately started to cry because I noticed my own growth in this moment. I was really finished. I was really finished with a book that I told God no to just eight months ago. I had really done it. I had sat, in obedience, and wrote out my story of faith. I sent a voice memo back in tears saying,

"Giving birth to my baby. Oh, Sarah I'm about

to cry [inserts cracking voice and sobs here]. Hold on. There's so much blood, sweat, and tears [deep sigh while crying] that went behind this book. Some people will never understand the words that are on that paper and what all I went through to get to where I am. Oh, Glory [inserts deep crying sob here]! Oh God I thank you [inserts loud cry here]. I thank you Lord. Thank you."

After I sent the voice memo, it all came back to my memory that this time seven years ago was so pivotal. At this very moment, seven years ago, I had just found out that I was pregnant with my first born. It was the moment where I learned that my plans were truly being interrupted. Seven years ago, around this same time, I had received the very promise I am speaking of in this book. Thinking about that broken, confused, disappointed, lost woman from seven years ago who is now whole, content, at peace, and writing a book about the entire experience makes me cry tears of joy. The best thing about it all is I went through this journey with the same person who invited me to church where I received the promise.

God reconnected us in the beginning of 2019. We have been here for each other throughout our journeys in 2019. We have laughed, prayed, cried, and stood in the gap for each other throughout these eight months. We have carried each other in faith. This has been a true Mary and Elizabeth moment. She has been my spiritual sister, prayer warrior, faith speaker, and, most importantly, my constant reminder of what God said. I am not sure I could have gone through this journey without her. Sarah, thank you!

To you, the woman who is reading this book, I want to first tell you that you are enough. Whatever God has placed on your heart to do, DO IT! I can't stress it to you enough that God has a reason for everything and He will make room for you. Initially, I didn't want to start a blog because everyone has one. I didn't want to write a book because everyone is writing one. With both assignments I delayed my obedience. Even when it does not seem to make sense and it doesn't seem to line up with where you are now, God has a plan. Sis, get in the birthing position and get ready to birth what God has placed on the inside of you. Right now you may be feeling labor pains but that just means it is time to push. It is time for you push through pain and birth out the purpose. Let God do for you what He did for me!

John 16:20-24
I tell you the truth, you will weep and mourn over what is going to happen to me, but the world will rejoice. You will grieve, but your grief will suddenly turn to wonderful joy. It will be like a woman suffering the pains of labor. When her child is born, her anguish gives way to joy because she has brought a new baby into the world. So you have sorrow now, but I will see you again; then you will rejoice, and no one can rob you of that joy. At that time you won't need to ask me for anything. I tell you the truth, you will ask the Father directly, and he will grant your request because you use my name. You haven't done this before. Ask, using my name, and you will receive, and you will have abundant joy.

The Seven Year Promise

About the Author

LaTasha Houston is an author, businesswoman, writer, and dynamic speaker from Mississippi. She is a newbie to the Rocket City—Huntsville, AL. A federal government worker by day and a writer by night (and weekends), she is on a mission to hug every woman and whisper to her "God is going to heal that, God can mend that, and He is going to fix that!"

After graduating from high school, LaTasha attended Jackson State University (JSU), where she studied Public Relations with a minor in English. LaTasha went on to obtain a Masters in Public Administration. She regularly blogs on her website www.biblicallyledcornbreadfed.com. The "Biblically Led" is LaTasha's testament of being led by God and the "Cornbread Fed" resounds her love for the south. She has a love for empowering women to own their imperfections and leading women to Christ, which she regularly blogs about. Once being full of shame from past decisions, she aims to get women from a place of focusing on perfection and, instead, aim for purpose. With her messages of owning your imperfections, she has a unique way of sharing the gospel in a relatable and distinctive way. She is often sought out by her family, friends, and others for her unwavering desire to encourage and live out God's word.

When she is not pursuing her career and ministry endeavors, LaTasha enjoys spending time with family, especially her two children, listening to music, and traveling. She is a devoted Christian and mom.

Stay Connected

Go check out my blog:
www.bibilicallyledcornbreadfed.com

Join the conversation on Facebook:
https://www.facebook.com/biblicallyledcornbreadfed/

Follow on Instagram:
https://www.instagram.com/biblicallyledcornbreadfed/

www.ingramcontent.com/pod-product-compliance
Lightning Source LLC
Chambersburg PA
CBHW031147160426
43193CB00008B/286